IMAGES
of America

DRY FALLS AND SUN LAKES

Every year, thousands of people stop at Sun Lakes–Dry Falls State Park, where they have an opportunity to learn about the geology of the immense Dry Falls and, in turn, the creation of the Grand Coulee. Dry Falls sits at the heart of the Grand Coulee, balanced between the Upper Coulee and the Lower Coulee, surrounded by a land defined partly by the people who briefly passed through. Pictured here from left to right are Michael W. Straus, commissioner of the US Bureau of Reclamation, pointing toward the Bacon Siphon, with Grand Coulee Dam chief engineer Frank A. Banks and US secretary of the interior Julius Albert Krug standing on the lookout at Dry Falls. (Courtesy Grant County Historical Museum.)

ON THE COVER: The overlook at the Vista House at Dry Falls stands over 400 feet above where the cataclysmic floods roared into the Lower Coulee, creating a chain of lakes that once flowed toward Soap Lake. Dry for centuries, the waterfall has been a unique stop for hundreds of thousands of people and an inspiration to many of them. (Author's collection.)

IMAGES
of America

Dry Falls and Sun Lakes

John M. Kemble

ARCADIA
PUBLISHING

Published by Arcadia Publishing
Charleston, South Carolina

Printed in the United States of America

Library of Congress Control Number: 2021930783

For all general information, please contact Arcadia Publishing:
Telephone 843-853-2070
Fax 843-853-0044
E-mail sales@arcadiapublishing.com
For customer service and orders:
Toll-Free 1-888-313-2665

Visit us on the Internet at www.arcadiapublishing.com

This book is for everyone.

CONTENTS

ACKNOWLEDGMENTS

Thanks to Steamboat Rock, Dry Falls, and Umatilla for being so amazing.

Extra special thanks go to Birdie Hensley and the Coulee Pioneer Museum; Pat Witham and the great people at the Grant County Historical Museum; David McWalters and the Dry Falls Interpretive Center; Jim and Jeanie Ping at Sun Lakes Park Resort; Alicia Woods, Brain Thrasher, and Alex McMurry at the Washington State Parks and Recreation Commission; Dan Bolyard; Michael Lehmann; Suzy and Wes Perkinson; Elizabeth Palachuk; Jerry Isenhart; Bert Smith; Samuel F. Taschereau; Dennis King; Dani Bolyard; Goldey Moyer; and Chuck Allen.

Big thanks go to these amazing people: Nora Egger, Art Brown, Warren Bolyard, Bruce Bjornstad, Tracey and Mike McMillian, Zach Kellams, Don Bluth, Chuck Flint, R.T. Williams, and Debra A. Mahon.

Special thanks to Jovanka Ristic and Susan M. Peschel at the American Geographical Society, Dennis King Photography, Them Dam Writers online, Washington State Digital Archive, Library of Congress, US Bureau of Reclamation, Grant County PUD, University of Wisconsin, the Special Collections Research Center University of Chicago Library, and of course, Sun Lakes–Dry Falls State Park.

Thanks to Jacque Warner for the fun at work and Stacia Bannerman and the great people at Arcadia Publishing for insight and wisdom.

Finally, extra special thanks to the Lake Chelan Museum, home of the L.D. Lindsley Collection, as well as my grandparents Jean and Oral Willard for taking so many amazing photographs.

INTRODUCTION

The story of Dry Falls and Sun Lakes begins at Dry Falls, a unique landscape that has inspired people into greatness for generations. The world's largest extinct waterfall, a place where over centuries the waters of the Columbia River cascaded down into the Lower Coulee, slowly washing away at a waterfall that started near where Soap Lake is today. Finally, over time, a huge coulee was created, the Grand Coulee. To cut such a huge gap in the solid basalt took centuries. The story of Dry Falls and Sun Lakes is a story of persistence, of blurred timelines, going against the grain to create something new, and carving rock with water. This is the story of the people who were inspired by the massive Dry Falls and how, out of the barren rock and disbelief of others, they created new legends and, in the case of J Harlen Bretz, redefined the study of geology on a global scale.

The story begins in the last ice age, during the late Pleistocene epoch. The land around the Dry Falls area was choked with huge glaciers; one, the Okanogan Lobe, stretched from where Highway 2 is today west of Coulee City all the way up into Canada. Below the huge melting glacier periodically ran the diverted Columbia River in a low valley. Uncounted times over the ensuing centuries, huge ice dams as far north as Montana would suddenly burst and send cataclysmic floods crashing down the Columbia River, where they were diverted into the ancient Columbia River bed, tearing out huge chunks of basalt and creating what we today call the Grand Coulee. But nobody really knew that for a long time. It was J Harlin Bretz who first explained this idea to a group of his peers, only to be ridiculed. It was believed that the Grand Coulee walls were created from erosion caused by melting glaciers, and that was the accepted scientific explanation. It took a long time for evidence of the massive floods to bob to the surface. There is now ample evidence that unimaginable floods violently tore through the earth and solid basalt, ripping a huge coulee unlike anything else on earth, nearly 60 miles long from the Columbia River to Soap Lake, sometimes as wide as five miles. The torrential waters traveled at times as fast as 75 miles per hour and were up to 400 feet deep, as deep as Dry Falls itself. The massive flood carried granite and basalt debris that was scattered along the route and eventually washed down into the Ephrata area.

An enormous prehistoric waterfall started around Soap Lake. Over the centuries the waterfall started to deteriorate, causing it to recede up the flood canal, eating away at the coulee until it reached its current location, Dry Falls. The waterfall and catastrophic floods wore away at the basalt and granite for centuries. The coulee took a more familiar shape toward the end of the flooding; the water started to fan out around the Coulee City area before plunging over the edge of a 400-foot-deep, three-mile-wide waterfall collectively known today as Dry Falls, consisting of Deep Lake, Monument Coulee, and the Dry Falls Cataract, as well as two side tributary cataracts. At Dry Falls, the diverted Columbia River ran periodically as the last ice age slowly came grinding to an end and the planet warmed. Some water became trapped in the Lower Grand Coulee, forming a chain of lakes as the last of the glaciers receded into Canada. The chain of lakes starts at the base of the falls with Dry Falls Lake and continues down the Lower Coulee, ending with Soap Lake. When the waters and ice finally receded and dried up, a low, easy-to-access spot was left standing in the area where Highway 2 runs today, which bridged the gap and also was a halfway point between Upper and Lower Coulee. At one time, this area sat beneath the Okanogan Ice Lobe that carried in Pilot Rock, and saw the massive floodwaters fan out below it. Dry Falls was less than two miles to the south, in clear view.

This area was discovered by early travelers as an easy way across the Grand Coulee and later was used by fur trappers and gold miners. It became referred to as the middle pass. The path was probably used by the indigenous people long before the settlers, and before that, it was most likely a game trail for centuries. This low spot provided easy access from the Waterville Plateau to the Hartline Plateau. Even though there were other places to cross the Grand Coulee, this was the easiest and safest place to cross with a wagon or stagecoach. Many of the travelers headed to the middle pass were guided by Pilot Rock, sitting high on the landscape where it was deposited by the Okanogan Lobe or some other prehistoric geological occurrence. Pilot Rock guided travelers and stagecoaches for decades before becoming obsolete as an aid to navigation. The middle pass continued to be used by many people and evolved with the times. As cars became more prevalent, the middle pass slowly evolved into the Sunset Highway, which by 1910 connected the Dry Falls area with Seattle to the west and eventually Spokane to the east.

In the farming days of the early 1900s, Dry Falls gained recognition as an obstacle that had to be circumvented to get to the lakes at its base. Early settlers found the freshwater lakes at the bottom of Dry Falls and started setting up farms, cattle ranches, and orchards there. The easiest way to get into the Lower Coulee was down the Cariboo Trail, which was used by wagons as well as early cars. Farmers in the Lower Coulee around Park Lake and Deep Lake used the Cariboo Trail to get their goods to market, to the train, or to pick up supplies in Coulee City. Another route out of the Blue Lake area involved going over the High Hill toward Pinto Ridge.

As time passed, a road system was created to link all the lakes in the Lower Coulee. Later, a route up the side of the coulee wall and past Dry Falls connected with the Sunset Highway. The coming of the automobiles brought new types of people to the coulee, and like the waters that once roared down the Big Bend, a flood of people now made that trek. Auto camps soon became resorts, with a couple on Blue and Park Lakes in the Lower Coulee. The resort owners of the 1920s and 1930s in the Lower Coulee built their resorts close to the newly established road system and offered lakeside cabins to traveling salesmen and other people venturing through the area.

Some people claim that this is where Victor Meyers got the idea for Sun Lakes, from the resorts and cabins along the highway in the Lower Coulee. Like J Harlen Bretz before him, Vic Meyers stood against adversity in the belief of his vision of Sun Lakes State Park, a vacation wonderland in the middle of a desert. This book tells the story of how all these elements and more have flowed together and had as much impact on the land and people as the unimaginable floods of the prehistoric ages.

One

FARMS, CARS, AND COULEE CITY

On the east side of the middle pass was Coulee City. In the early 1900s it was a railhead, dropping off travelers headed further into the Okanogan region or down the coulee to Seaton's Landing. The streets were dirt and lined with businesses in wooden buildings. The train was the lifeline for many settlers, bringing in supplies and travelers while taking livestock and wheat to far off markets. (Courtesy Dan Bolyard.)

Coulee City was in a prime location, with freshwater springs and ample land for grazing; it also sat on both a well-used passenger rail line and stagecoach route. Early in the 1900s, the area was settled by ranchers who took advantage of the train to send their products to market. (Courtesy Coulee Pioneer Museum.)

It was because of the train that Coulee City began to grow with saloons, livery stables, gambling halls, and perhaps the biggest attraction of them all, the stagecoach out of town. To many people, Coulee City was just a stop or a place to do business, not a final destination. (Courtesy Coulee Pioneer Museum.)

The wide-open plains and bunch grass that first served the cattle ranchers prior to the 20th century were slowly taken over by fences and wheat. Soon, the train was transporting more wheat than cattle from Coulee City in the ever-changing times. (Author's collection.)

During harvest season, the town would fill up with hired help from around the county and beyond. Coulee City could at times feel like a Wild West town suited for filming a Hollywood movie, but most of the time, the dust hardly seemed to move. (Courtesy Coulee Pioneer Museum.)

Frank McCann had been to the region when he was younger, working on one of Phillip McEntee's harvesting crews, and fell in love with the landscape, promising himself he would return and learn everything he could about the region. It was a promise he kept when he returned to Coulee City in 1902 with a better education and money to invest. (Courtesy Coulee Pioneer Museum.)

NO 29-MAIN STREET, LOOKING SOUTH, COULEE WN.

McCann, along with a business partner, opened a general store in Coulee City and offered farming equipment on credit. At the time, credit was a new idea and not very well regulated. Using his social influence, Frank McCann entered into politics, at times becoming a one-man chamber of commerce. (Courtesy Michael Lehmann.)

Automobiles had been around in America since the late 1890s, but production was slow, and not many people had them. A bigger deal for the farming regions at the turn of the 20th century was the advent of mechanized farming equipment and the newly established system of buying on credit. (Courtesy Coulee Pioneer Museum.)

Frank McCann loved Dry Falls and spent his time out among the sagebrush and basalt exploring. It was not long before he became a local expert on the area. He had taken a geology class and applied his knowledge to his observations in the coulee. (Author's collection.)

It was during this time that McCann started using his influence to draw attention to Dry Falls and the possibility of making it into a park. What some called a "damn hole in the ground," McCann considered of national worth and started inviting prominent geologists down into the coulee to look at its unique features. (Author's collection.)

One hot, dry day in 1912, a caravan of automobiles pulled up into Coulee City late in the afternoon. It was the Transcontinental Excursion of 1912. The group was comprised of people from all over the world who rapidly made their way across the United States under the supervision and itinerary of noted geologist William Morris Davis. (Courtesy the American Geographical Society Library, University of Wisconsin Milwaukee Libraries.)

Earlier in the day, the Transcontinental Excursion had enjoyed lunch in the shadow of Steamboat Rock prepared by the George Baldwin family, who also took photographs of the historic event. For many of the excursionists, it was their first time in America and first taste of the culture. (Courtesy Coulee Pioneer Museum.)

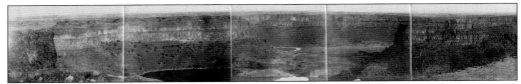

By the end of the day, the caravan had pushed down past the Columbia Basin Orchard and into Coulee City for a quick stop at Dry Falls and one of the earliest-known photographs of the extinct waterfall. The members of the excursion came from all walks of life, but most were scientists and geologists. (Courtesy the American Geographical Society Library, University of Wisconsin Milwaukee Libraries.)

Some of the members of the excursion were artists and drew what they saw, while others brought cameras. Even in 1912, Dry Falls called out to people's imaginations. The day was growing short when the excursion boarded the train out of Coulee City to its next destination. (Courtesy Willard family.)

In 1913, Henry Ford started using assembly line procedures to mass-produce affordable cars for the public. This was a historic turning point for American culture; as more and more people bought automobiles, it was becoming evident that this new freedom would change the country and open up places less frequently visited. (Courtesy Ford Motor Company.)

Assembly line production lowered the cost of automobiles, and suddenly, most people could afford cars. People would drive anywhere; there were a few roads, but there were more wagon trails and wide-open spaces to be traveled and explored. (Author's collection.)

The year 1913 is also when Washington State created the Board of Park Commissioners, whose job it was to take control of the acquisition of lands donated or otherwise received by the state for the purpose of state parks. Without a clearly established direction, the system worked slowly at first. (Courtesy Coulee Pioneer Museum.)

One of the reasons that state spending was allocated and the Board of Park Commissioners created was that the government believed that parks directly affected peoples' mental health. The country was making a transition into more urban settings, and the government believed more people could seek solace in parks, leading to an overall healthier society. (Author's collection.)

By 1920, Frank McCann heard of the plan to irrigate with water dammed at the Columbia River 30 miles away. He jumped on the bandwagon and started promoting the dam to anyone who would listen—even investing his own capital when needed. (Author's collection.)

In 1921, the newly reformed State Parks Committee gave the state the authority to create and regulate its own parks, including the generation of funds and acquisition of land. While campaigning for the Grand Coulee Dam, Frank McCann started using his influence to draw attention to Dry Falls and the possibility of making it into a state park. (Author's collection.)

19

By the Roaring Twenties, most of the country was living high on the hog, celebrating the end of World War I and a prospering economy. The Grand Coulee, however, slumped into a recession caused by the end of the war and a local drought that seemed to last forever. (Courtesy Michael Lehmann.)

Coulee City became a town at a crossroads, with people passing through and locals with too much invested in the land to give up, even during the hard times. Still a bustling town, the advent of the automobile made the stagecoach obsolete and the train less important. (Courtesy Dan Bolyard.)

Two

PARKS, DRY FALLS, AND POSTCARDS

Between 1920 and 1930, cars started to become common, and everyone seemed to own one. The states worked feverishly building and improving roads. At the same time, states started building parks to give the people places to go. The Washington State Parks Committee believed that parks were needed to help maintain a healthy society, and more and more, automobiles and roads determined where parks would be located. The connection between cars, parks, and roads was established. In 1920, the federal government turned over 30,000 acres to Washington State in the Dry Falls and Park Lake area. (Author's collection.)

Always an energetic and vocal supporter, Frank McCann finally saw one of his lifelong pursuits become a reality when the State Parks Committee voted to turn Dry Falls into a state park. The park was planned out, and construction was started. (Courtesy Dry Falls Interpretive Center.)

The road that led to the new Dry Falls State Park was just a rock throw from the busy Sunset Highway between Seattle and Spokane. It was the Roaring Twenties, and people wanted to get out and hit the road in their automobiles. (Author's collection.)

56- Vesta House, Built of different Rock Formations found in Grand Coulee. Dry Falls State Park, (C) DeLong.

At the time of this stone gazebo's creation, the state's primary design goal was to reflect the surroundings while adding beauty and functionality without compromising natural aesthetics. The gazebo was created with stones collected from within the Grand Coulee. On top was a wood shingled roof with a star-like ornament pointing in all directions. (Author's collection.)

The opening-day ceremony at Dry Falls State Park in 1928 drew people from all over Upper and Lower Coulee, as well as the media and officials. Speakers included Rufus Woods, Frank McCann, and geologist J Harlen Bretz, who had been conducting field studies in the area. (Courtesy Samuel F. Taschereau.)

The park was dedicated to the people of Washington on July 25, 1928. The Almira chapter of Boy Scouts were on hand to act as guides, the Vista House was christened with water from the Columbia River, the Wenatchee American Legion raised the flag, and the Manson Band played "America." (Courtesy Dan Bolyard.)

For a while, there were no stone pillars or chain as seen in later pictures; the only thing that stopped people from falling over the 400-foot drop was common sense. Eventually, it became apparent that that was not going to be enough, and chained pillars were added. (Author's collection.)

The Vista House offered shelter from rain or snow, and in the center was an information kiosk with some facts about Dry Falls, as well as a noticeboard for current affairs, a guestbook for visitors to sign, and several displays. The guestbook was open for the public to read as well, and with entries from all over the country and beyond, became a favorite of visitors. (Author's collection.)

In the 1930s, "Vista House" was a common name; "vista" referred to the panoramic view, and the view from inside the house certainly lived up to its name. What began as a generic name that was more a description over time became the formal name of the building. (Author photograph.)

The construction crew took advantage of a natural stone outcropping and built a fenced sidewalk on top of it to allow for a better view into the chasm below. From here, visitors can look out over several lakes and prominent land features. (Author photograph.)

For most people at the time, the chance to be 400 feet up in the air was unique and quite thrilling. Children would dare each other to walk out to the end, even though it was perfectly safe. At the time of its construction and for many years afterward, the walkway tested the nerve of many visitors. (Author photograph.)

From the catwalk, one becomes immersed in Dry Falls, and it becomes hard to imagine that this was once a great waterfall, perhaps the largest in the world, because of its immense size. The cataract floor is a breathtaking 400 feet down, through a basalt talus slope into sagebrush and cheatgrass. (Author's collection.)

The huge rock in the center of Dry Falls is known as Umatilla, but that was not always so. The north end that sits above Dry Falls Lake was once called "the Sphinx," named after the famous figure in Egypt, which it resembles when viewed from the side, especially at sunset. (Author photograph.)

The south end was known as Battleship Rock because of its shape and perhaps the "wake" composed of a basalt talus slope. The center part of the almost mile-long rock formation is usually forgotten by photographers. Altogether, it makes what is called Umatilla on maps and by locals. (Author photograph.)

An old legend that was passed around the Dry Falls area was the story of Chief Umatilla. He sat high on top of the mesa, saying his prayers and making the other chiefs jealous. Together, the opposing chiefs conjured up a giant lizard and sent it after Chief Umatilla. Halfway up the mesa, the lizard stiffened up and turned to stone due to Chief Umatilla's powerful prayers. The lizard can still be seen frozen in time and stone where he took his last step. (Courtesy Washington State Parks and Recreation Commission, 156-0-2014-1-29-6.)

Eventually, Battleship Rock and the Sphinx were considered one rock, with the name Umatilla. Many postcards were taken of the Sphinx and Battleship Rock, but those names slowly started to phase out, as state-printed brochures made use of the new name. (Courtesy Coulee Pioneer Museum.)

On the west side of Umatilla sits Perch Lake. The small freshwater lake is named after the type of fish that were once stocked there. Before that, it was surrounded by waterfowl, providing early travelers with food and water. (Courtesy Grant County Historical Museum.)

At the bottom of all three of the major cataracts of Dry Falls sits a lake. In Dry Falls Coulee, at the base of the falls sits Dry Falls Lake. It has had several names over the years, including Basin Lake and Falls Lake. (Author's collection.)

Sitting out in Dry Falls Lake like a half-submerged predator is an island named Alligator Rock (or Alligator Head Rock), a popular subject for many postcards and photographs. (Author's collection.)

From the new state park could be clearly seen a dry waterfall more than three miles wide, containing several lakes and independent side coulees, as well as some of the most unique landscapes in the West. (Courtesy Grant County Historical Museum.)

Standing tall in the center of Dry Falls, Umatilla separates the west cataract from the one directly behind it. The cataract behind Umatilla is known as Monument Coulee, most likely due to the large erratics and massive chunks of basalt torn off from the surrounding walls that litter the coulee floor. (Courtesy Grant County Historical Museum.)

Monument Coulee is home to two seasonal lakes, Green Lake and Red Alkali Lake. Both are in the very back of the cataract and traditionally have been pretty rugged, attracting more hikers and nature enthusiasts than fishermen. (Author photograph.)

The farthest cataract from the Dry Falls parking lot and almost out of view is the Deep Lake cataract. This is the longest cataract and contains a massive lake. Full of legends and lore, Deep Lake is an almost magical place that seems to tell its own tales. (Courtesy Wes and Suzy Perkinson.)

The southernmost end of the Deep Lake cataract has an incline as it rises up out of the coulee and makes its way to the top of the wall. This is the Dan Paul Draw, which was once used by a Coulee City pioneer as a homestead and a route down to the lake. (Courtesy Grant County Historical Museum.)

In September 1928, a newly elected Washington governor made good on his campaign promise to reduce the cost of government spending and lighten the burden of taxation. In doing so, funding was cut off from state parks during his four years in office. (Courtesy Wes and Suzy Perkinson.)

During this time, the construction of Dry Falls State Park came to a halt, with only a few stone pillars finished. This is how the park would stay for several years, half-constructed and hardly maintained, with its future in limbo. Despite being unfinished, it was still a popular place for both travelers and locals and became a complete success, enjoyed by many people. (Courtesy Bert Smith.)

Dry Falls State Park happened to sit on a road and attracted tourists and anyone traveling the length of the Grand Coulee. Even though the park was closed, it was still a place to pull over, get out of the car, take in the amazing view, and learn a few things about the area. (Courtesy Washington State Parks and Recreation Commission, 156-0-2014-1-29-3.)

Around this time, postcards became popular. People had cars, but not everyone had a camera, and postcards were often inexpensive and imaginative, making them the number-one souvenir for many decades. (Courtesy Michael Lehmann.)

Many fledgling postcard companies sprung up in Washington State. One of the more well-known photographers was J. Boyd Ellis from Arlington, Washington. A one-time schoolteacher with a change of heart, Ellis started his own family business with a camera, car, and inspiration. With gas, money, and film, Ellis traveled around taking pictures and preserving history for decades. (Courtesy Coulee Pioneer Museum.)

SUN LAKES STATE PARK - GRAND COULEE OF WASHINGTON

Pretty soon, postcards of Dry Falls State Park, Deep Lake, Park Lake, the Vista House, and the lookout were flooding the tourist market from Soap Lake to Grand Coulee Dam, and could be bought in gas stations, souvenir shops, cafes, and any little store with a bit of space at the counter. (Courtesy Willard family.)

Not only did postcards encourage people from all walks of life to travel and see Dry Falls themselves, they also started a local industry, with a lot of photographers making their way down the coulee to get pictures of Alligator Rock, Battleship Rock, or the Sphinx. (Courtesy Willard family.)

Sometime during the 1930s, famed Washington photographer L.D. Lindsley traveled down into the Grand Coulee. Like most, he was probably first attracted to the Grand Coulee Dam project but found something special in the rugged beauty of the area. (Courtesy Jerry Isenhart.)

Lindsley's interest in the Grand Coulee shines through in his photographs from the area, as do his actions. Talking to locals, he spent time around Dry Falls, traveling out into the brush to photograph local landmarks and spots he considered interesting. (Courtesy Michael Lemann.)

One of the places Lindsley photographed was the Jumble Field in Monument Coulee. It is hard to say where Lindsley heard the name of this field of erratics and broken basalt or the significance he saw in it when he took his pictures. (Author photograph.)

Another rare landmark Lindsley photographed was Packhorse Rock. Lindsley traveled the bush taking pictures of these little-known landmarks. He would usually stay around the Park Lake area in the Lower Coulee, talking to locals and gathering information. (Author photograph.)

L.D. Lindsley took a certain interest in Deep Lake, one of the Dry Falls cataracts, and spent time exploring the area thoroughly. He returned to Deep Lake over and over, photographing it from the shore as well as from boats. (Courtesy Michael Lehmann.)

Over the years, he would return time and again from his Seattle home to take pictures of the Dry Falls and Park Lake areas. Lindsley's photographs preserve views that have been lost to time and the changing world, helping to define the past. (Courtesy Willard family.)

Three

GEOLOGY AND THE LOWER COULEE

The Lower Coulee stretches from the Dry Falls drop pool to the Soap Lake area, where the great receding waterfall that created Dry Falls started its slow northern march. In contrast with the Upper Coulee, where Coulee City is located, the Lower Coulee contained a string of lakes that attracted settlers and entrepreneurs. (Courtesy Coulee Pioneer Museum.)

Frank McCann had a small beach on a strip of land on Blue Lake, where it met Park Lake in the Lower Coulee. There, he had a public beach as well as a few cabins and a ranch house. He would allow the public to have events on McCann's Beach, and it soon became well known around the coulee. (Author's collection.)

Frank McCann had a love of the Grand Coulee and believed that one day it would be recognized as one of the true marvels of the world. Early on, he started inviting geologists to his beachfront property and then go out on walks with them, observing the landscape and exchanging notes. (Courtesy Coulee Pioneer Museum.)

WALINGER

One of those who visited McCann's beach was famed geologist J Harlen Bretz. The two would discuss geology and travel around the coulee, collecting samples and making observations. McCann became a believer in and advocate for Bretz's then-controversial theories. (Courtesy the Special Collections Research Center, University of Chicago Library.)

Bretz's explanations and reputation became just as solid as the basalt and granite his study was made of, but not right away. At first, his ideas met with opposition from the geology field. From around 1920 through 1931, Bretz visited the Grand Coulee area, often conducting field studies with Frank McCann. (Courtesy Coulee Pioneer Museum.)

J Harlen Bretz believed the Grand Coulee was created by a cataclysmic flood, evidence for which lay all around the coulee and beyond. He coined the term "channeled scablands" to describe the area and named several local landmarks, including the Blade, seen here. (Author photograph.)

DRY FALLS
GRAND COULEE - WASHINGTON

For a long time, the accepted thinking had been that the Grand Coulee was created by the slow melting of glaciers over a long period of time like other similar coulees and canyons. This explanation for Dry Falls was even printed on the back of the 1928 dedication ceremony program where J Harlen Bretz spoke. (Courtesy Grant County Historical Museum.)

Despite the common belief, Bretz theorized that the Grand Coulee was created by a massive flood, or perhaps a series of floods. However, he lacked the evidence to prove it. What started as a geological debate became a philosophical debate about uniformitarianism, the idea that similar circumstances universally create similar outcomes. Bretz's ideas challenged the whole geological community. (Courtesy Grant County Historical Museum.)

J Harlen Bretz's radical ideas inspired people to come to the Grand Coulee and look at the evidence themselves. With automobiles and developing road systems, a new age of rockhound came to the Grand Coulee. (Courtesy Coulee Pioneer Museum.)

Great meetings of geologists were held on McCann's Beach; in 1933, Frank McCann hosted a party of 40 geologists for J Harlen Bretz. It was the International Geographical Congress, with members from five continents and 22 nations. (Author's collection.)

Bretz was absent but asked McCann to lead the group on a tour, which he did. They toured Dry Falls, then down to Blue Lake, where McCann had his private beach area, and on to Lake Lenore, Soap Lake, Ephrata, and Adrian, while looking at evidence of Bretz's great floods. (Courtesy Coulee Pioneer Museum.)

The group later met on the Coulee City schoolhouse lawn to talk about the changes that were coming to the region due to the construction of the Grand Coulee Dam, which had not started yet. Pertinent facts were explained by a chief of the US Army Corps of Engineers, in the area doing preliminary survey work for the dam. (Courtesy Michael Lehmann.)

J Harlen Bretz's 1932 book, *The Grand Coulee*, sparked the imagination of the public, sending amateur rockhounds as well as seasoned professional geologists pouring into the Grand Coulee searching for evidence of Bretz's flood and examining the scablands firsthand. It was not until much later that evidence was finally found, proving Bretz's theories. (Author's collection.)

Close to McCann's Beach was Jasper Cove, a place rich with lore; it included an area that became known and advertised as the Fossil Beds. Promoted as a place for tourists to visit and explore, it was added to local road maps, and many people visited. (Courtesy Grant County PUD.)

17- View taken from Cavity where Vertical Petrified Tree stood. Blue Lake, Grand Coulee. © DeLong & Drake.

This is where a prehistoric swamp full of trees and wildlife was covered by a flow of lava. Like the lava cave in Dry Falls, the trees became petrified wood, leaving long, tree-shaped holes. Other fossils could be found as well, like shells and castings. (Courtesy Wes and Suzy Perkinson.)

At a time before most people considered artifact preservation, and in order to drive up tourism, people were allowed to take parts of the fossils they found home as souvenirs. A couple of rockhounds vacationing at Soap Lake and searching the Fossil Beds for petrified wood discovered the famous Rhino Cave of Blue Lake. (Author photograph.)

Both the Fossil Beds and the Blue Lake Rhino Cave were in Jasper Cove, and soon there was a ferry system of small motorboats to take people to visit these tourist attractions. As time passed, fossils from the Fossil Beds disappeared into people's homes. The Rhino Cave fared better and was excavated mostly by local universities. (Courtesy Willard family.)

By 1936, a paved highway ran from Soap Lake to the base of Dry Falls that was an extension of State Road 7. The goal was to link State Road 7, also known as the North Central Highway, with State Road 2, the Sunset Highway. Part of the reason for this was to help expedite movement of people and materials to the Grand Coulee Dam construction site, but mostly it was just another example of the evolving and expanding road system at the time. (Author's collection.)

Park Lake Wn. 43.

The media called it the Scenic Highway, a well-used gimmicky nickname, and the highway was certainly breathtaking. Leaving Soap Lake, the road traveled north to where it crossed Lake Lenore and on to the west side of Blue Lake, where it once more shifted east to run along Park Lake and up a switchback to the Upper Coulee. (Author's collection.)

Before ascending the hill, sitting on the beach was the Park Lake Resort, which had cabins, a washroom, a café, and a gas station. In the 1930s, no one thought about fuel economy, and gas cost on average 20¢ a gallon. There was also a small farm or two dotting the area, creating a small, tight-knit community. (Courtesy Dan Bolyard.)

Four

DRY FALLS, FDR, AND THE WPA

Shortly after the construction of the Vista House in 1928, the Great Depression struck, and construction on state parks halted until the landslide 1932 election of Franklin D. Roosevelt. Clarence Martin was also elected governor of Washington, and one of his first acts was to start construction and maintenance of state parks. The same election saw Victor Aloysius Meyer become lieutenant governor—his name would come into play later. (Courtesy Library of Congress.)

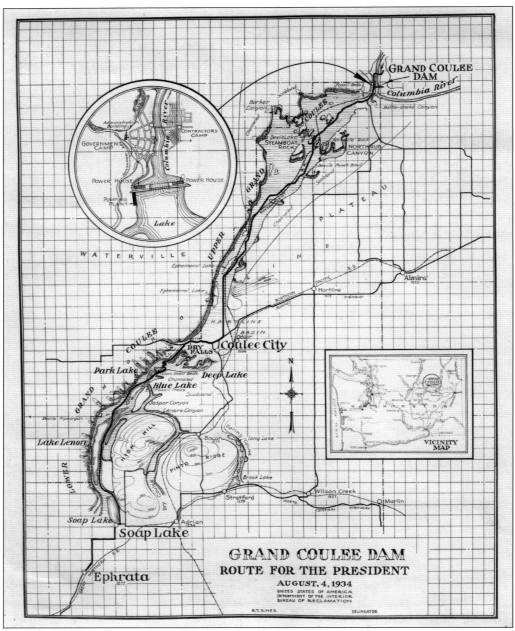

In August 1934, President Roosevelt made a trip down into the Grand Coulee to visit the fledgling Grand Coulee Dam. Roosevelt departed the train in Ephrata and boarded an automobile caravan that traveled down the newly created Scenic Highway through the Lower Coulee. In 1934, the Scenic Highway was still a gravel road and had to be oiled to keep the dust down as the president and his men passed through. On the itinerary was a scheduled stop at Dry Falls State Park. (Courtesy Grant County Historical Museum.)

In 1934, the Grand Coulee Dam project had just barely started, and most of the visible work was excavation. In order to build the dam, a huge hill had to come down, and everything just looked like a huge pile of dirt, with men and trucks scurrying around. The president was ferried over the river and viewed the construction from the east side. (Courtesy Coulee Pioneer Museum.)

A huge stage was set up about where downtown Grand Coulee is now, in a natural auditorium, as the papers called it, and people came from all over to hear the president speak. Two years later, Roosevelt signed the bill to continue work and create the high dam to irrigate the Columbia Basin. (Courtesy Coulee Pioneer Museum.)

To combat the Great Depression that was ravaging the country, in 1935, President Roosevelt unveiled the second part of the New Deal, which introduced the Works Progress Administration (WPA). The idea was to provide jobs instead of soup lines, and it became responsible for creating everything from public buildings to parks as well as promoting and financing the arts, education, and a healthy lifestyle. (Courtesy Library of Congress.)

The second part of the New Deal called for the improvement of national resources, which included the upkeep and creation of parks. Work had already been started on Dry Falls State Park shortly after Governor Martin took office in 1932. A labor camp had been set up in Dry Falls for transient workers during the Depression. (Courtesy Bert Smith.)

In early 1936, it was announced that the WPA would take over the labor camp in Dry Falls, and with an allotment of government money, construction on Dry Falls State Park continued. Work included trails, roadways, and groundskeeping, among other improvements. (Courtesy Washington State Parks and Recreation Commission, 156-0-2014-1-29-8.)

There was also a Civilian Conservation Corps group that had been active in the Grand Coulee area. It is likely that some of these boys got tangled up with the local WPA and also worked on Dry Falls. There was a general sense of unrest during the Depression, with people often traveling to seek work. (Courtesy Grant County Historical Museum.)

Dry Falls State Park was once more under construction, fueled by the New Deal; work was done by the WPA between 1936 and 1939, backed by the State Parks Committee. (Courtesy Coulee Pioneer Museum.)

The men who worked on Dry Falls during this time were an eclectic lot of skilled and non-skilled laborers from all over the country, like the tourists who visited Dry Falls on a regular basis. During the mid-1930s, the newly reconstructed Dry Falls saw a dramatic increase in visitors stopping by the Vista House and enjoying the lookout. (Courtesy Washington State Parks and Recreation Commission, 156-0-2014-1-29-1.)

By 1936, the visitor count at the Vista House was hitting record highs. Sometimes, tour buses pulled up, and people piled out. Even during one of the worst years of the Depression, the park was described as overflowing. The state had succeeded in creating a distraction from the stresses of a changing society. (Courtesy Washington State Parks and Recreation Commission, 156-0-2014-1-29-9.)

The reason for the sudden surge in tourists at Dry Falls was that a huge project had started to really get underway about 30 miles away at the Columbia River, the Grand Coulee Dam. The dam was also part of the New Deal and employed as many as 7,000 workers during the Great Depression. It was all a great spectacle and attracted bus tours that would often add Dry Falls to their list of stops as an added attraction. (Courtesy Willard family.)

Towns started springing up around the Grand Coulee Dam construction site and down the Grand Coulee itself toward Coulee City. Coulee City experienced a new growth spurt when it became a staging ground for people and materials headed down the coulee to the dam construction site. (Courtesy Coulee Pioneer Museum.)

Dry Falls State Park became a tourist spot for the workers on the Grand Coulee Dam as well as a stop for people traveling down the coulee. In the 1930s, the park's tourism grew almost daily in the summer, setting and breaking attendance records on almost a weekly basis during the tourist months. (Courtesy Michael Lehmann.)

The Grand Coulee Dam was a spectacle, the largest building project around for hundreds of miles, and tourists flocked to it. Dry Falls became a popular stop along the way, offering restrooms, water, and a spectacular, one-of-a-kind view. (Courtesy Grant County Historical Museum.)

The lookout at the Vista House offered people a small thrill as well as a great photo opportunity. From the walkway, all of the Dry Falls cataracts can be seen, including stunning landmarks like Umatilla and Dry Falls Lake, with the Alligator Head peering out of the blue water. (Courtesy Bert Smith.)

Following the guidance of both the WPA and the State Park Committee, the stone pillars were created in the same manner as the Vista House, with locally gathered rocks. The chain was stretched through them, and finally, the parking lot was completed. (Courtesy Bert Smith.)

One of the first groups to explore the new park were the Boy Scouts. Known for camping and outdoor trips, the Boy Scouts of Yakima discovered a cave in Dry Falls that was different from any cave in the region because it had stalactites and stalagmites. The cave drew the attention of the media, and soon, Ellensburg geologist George Beck and local expert Frank McCann, as well as park officials, declared the stalactites and stalagmites to be calcareous formations. (Courtesy Dani Bolyard.)

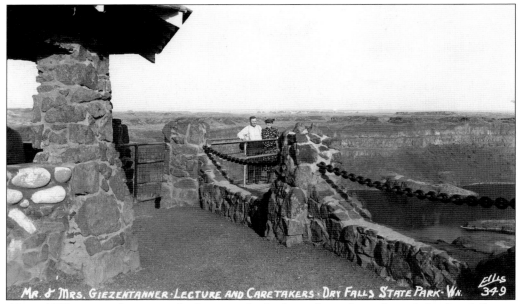

About 1935, a stone house was built across the highway from the park, and the first full-time interpretive specialist moved in. His name was C.T. Giezentanner, a lifelong newspaperman from Pasco, Washington; he often mixed poetry with his explanations of Dry Falls. (Courtesy Wes and Suzy Perkinson.)

Giezentanner lived with his wife in the stone house on the rim of Dry Falls. He was considered a romantic, always weaving classic literature into his explanations of Dry Falls. When the house was being built, C.T. wrote the story of his own romance, sealed it in a bottle, and trapped it in a stone wall of the house, where it remains today. (Author's collection.)

C.T. Giezentanner was so popular with tourists and locals that, for a while, he became something of an exhibit himself, with people arriving at Dry Falls solely to hear his lectures. He was so popular that postcards were made of him and sold next to the racks of souvenir postcards of Dry Falls. (Courtesy Wes and Suzy Perkinson.)

The Grand Coulee Dam was completed just as America entered World War II. Many of the men who had worked to build the dam went off to war, and other projects were left behind, slowed down, or placed on hold. After the war, people once more started to trickle back into the Grand Coulee, and work resumed on the plan to irrigate the dry farmlands by bringing water from the Columbia River south, just like in prehistoric times. (Courtesy Coulee Pioneer Museum.)

Five

BANKS LAKE AND THE BACON SIPHON

After World War II ended in 1945, work began on the second phase of the Grand Coulee Dam, which was irrigation. The plan was to pump Columbia River water up from behind the dam into canals to be transported to dry fields over 100 miles away. A majority of the Upper Coulee was turned into a 27-mile reservoir by filling it with water from the Grand Coulee Dam, about 30 miles to the north. (Courtesy Grant County Historical Museum.)

This brought a deluge of workers to the area in 1947, and once more, Coulee City started to buzz with activity and people. Just outside of town, the government erected a village of Quonset huts, and workers and their families moved in, with many of their children going to the local school. (Courtesy Coulee Pioneer Museum.)

With so many new students flooding the school, the administration had to act fast and turned more Quonset huts into classrooms for students. They were hot in the summer and cold in the winter, but classes were still held indoors all year. (Courtesy Grant County Historical Museum.)

Work began on the South Dam near Coulee City. This earthen-style dam was reinforced with a concrete center. It stretched 9,800 feet, almost two miles from Coulee City to the Waterville Plateau, and was 123 feet high. (Courtesy Coulee Pioneer Museum.)

South Dam was created to stop the waters of the Columbia River from once more flowing over Dry Falls. as they had for untold centuries and during the occasional mega floods that created the Grand Coulee in a torrent of cataclysms. (Courtesy Coulee Pioneer Museum.)

South Coulee Dam would have to hold the millions of gallons of water from flooding over Dry Falls and into the Lower Coulee, which was inhabited with resorts full of summer vacationers, as well as a few farms and homesteads. (Courtesy Coulee Pioneer Museum.)

The construction was not always smooth sailing; seen here is a bogged-down crane just south of Coulee City. The construction workers dealt with alkaline-laden mud as well as other hazards like rattlesnakes and extreme heat during the summer months. (Courtesy Coulee Pioneer Museum.)

Despite all the construction, the area around Dry Falls stayed pretty rugged. Cougars, bears, and bobcats, as well as countless species of birds, call the coulee home and are attracted to the water. Many of the workers came to love the vastness of the surroundings. (Courtesy Willard family.)

Further up by the city of Grand Coulee, North Dam was under construction where the main feeder canal emptied into Banks Lake; South Dam is where it emptied into the main canal, headed for destinations like Pasco and Quincey. (Courtesy Grant County Historical Museum.)

At the north end of the Banks Lake reservoir was North Dam, where the main feeder canal released the waters of the Columbia River into the reservoir. This dam was much shorter, measuring only 1,450 feet long, but taller at 145 feet tall. (Courtesy Coulee Pioneer Museum.)

Water filled the 27-mile-long reservoir that starts at North Dam near Electric City and flows down past the farmlands of Steamboat Rock to the foot of Coulee City, where it was stopped from following its prehistoric course by the South Dam. (Author's collection.)

Like in the distant past, water diverted from the Columbia River once more flowed in the dry Upper Coulee, only this time held in check by a dam of concrete and earth. The new proposed reservoir would not hold even a quarter of the water that raged through the same area during the creation of the Grand Coulee. (Author's collection.)

On the north side of the main canal under the South Dam, the ground was lowered to allow the water to flow more easily. This area would be completely underwater and create a huge current as the water bottlenecked and eventually passed through to dryer lands to the south. (Courtesy Coulee Pioneer Museum.)

South Dam was where the water left the Banks Lake reservoir into the main canal, headed for the barren lands south of Dry Falls. The water followed a network of canals that slowly distributed the water over millions of acres. (Courtesy Coulee Pioneer Museum.)

But first, the waters of the Columbia had to face the dry riverbed of the Deep Lake coulee and the Dan Paul Draw. To circumvent this obstacle, a huge tunnel was built in the Dan Paul Draw named the Bacon Siphon and Bacon Tunnel. The siphon, a giant tube, passed under the earth. (Courtesy Coulee Pioneer Museum.)

The Bacon Siphon moved the displaced water through a 1,000-foot-long tube and through the back of the Deep Lake Coulee, across the Dan Paul Draw. The water of the Columbia River then traveled 21 miles, including 2 miles in the Bacon Tunnel and 5.5 miles of waterway created by the Long Lake Dam. (Courtesy Coulee Pioneer Museum.)

With the construction of the main canal, the diverted waters from the Columbia River once more flowed south to drylands, as it did countless centuries ago. While all this was going on, hundreds of miles of different sizes of irrigation canals were also being constructed. (Courtesy Coulee Pioneer Museum.)

The South Dam is an earthen-style dam, with locally gathered basalt rock piled up on either side like a manmade talus slope, reflecting the natural aesthetics of the surrounding landscape. On top, a two-lane roadway was paved. (Courtesy Coulee Pioneer Museum.)

The Sunset Highway was diverted to the top of the earthen dam, approximately where the middle pass once was, allowing people safe and easy passage between the Hartline and Waterville Plateaus. (Courtesy Grant County Historical Museum.)

South Dam, as it was known by locals, opened on September 1, 1950, with fanfare. It was a beautiful fall day, and many people parked on the dam and enjoyed the festivities. (Author's collection.)

South Dam was renamed Dry Falls Dam. Now the only way for the waters of the Columbia River to escape the 27-mile-long reservoir is through Dry Falls Dam and the main canal that runs right under the highway linking east and west, Highway 2, once known as the Sunset Highway. (Author photograph.)

The crossroads where the Scenic Highway and the Sunset Highway met became known as Dry Falls Junction, and several entrepreneur types started businesses there. One was named after the famous landmark just miles away, and another that came later was created from a surplus Quonset hut—many people remember the Hut Café. (Courtesy Dan Bolyard.)

In 1950, the main work on the canals was finished, and the Upper Coulee was flooded with water diverted from the Columbia River. The equalizing reservoir was named after the Grand Coulee Dam's chief engineer, Frank Banks. (Courtesy Grant County Historical Museum.)

By September 1951, water was being pumped out the main feeder canal at North Dam, slowly filling up the equalizing reservoir and bringing Banks Lake to life, a 27-mile reservoir holding water pumped from behind the Grand Coulee Dam. (Courtesy Dan Bolyard.)

The main canal out of Banks Lake travels south and eventually empties in Billy Clapp Lake, another reservoir that holds irrigation waters as they slowly make their way south into the drylands. (Courtesy Grant County Historical Museum.)

The waterway was named Summer Falls, and soon, the State Parks Committee was at work building another park at the base of the thundering falls. (Courtesy Grant County Historical Museum.)

With the majority of work on the canal system and Bacon Siphon complete, the population of Coulee City once more started to decline, taking the local economy with it. Even before the first waters of Banks Lake lapped against the shores of Coulee City, the Quonset hut village had been removed. Some huts were sold, and others were moved to Soap Lake and used once more to house Columbia Basin Irrigation workers. (Courtesy Dan Bolyard.)

The economy took a turn in Coulee City, which went from a town flooded with workers all earning money to a town supported by a few local businesses and a new breed of recreationists drawn to the shores of the newly created Banks Lake and all it had to offer. (Courtesy Willard family.)

Once more, the waters of the Columbia River ran down past Dry Falls, only this time controlled by the Bacon Siphon; they pass harmlessly under the tip of Dry Falls out into the far reaches of the dry farmland where the first water was released at Pasco in the spring of 1952. (Courtesy Coulee Pioneer Museum.)

Now, the waters from the Columbia River and the Grand Coulee Dam irrigate thousands of acres of land as they start out from Billy Clapp Lake and travel through thousands of miles of canals to reach the end of the line at Potholes Reservoir. (Courtesy Coulee Pioneer Museum.)

The waters of the harnessed Columbia River brought life to the drylands of central Washington, but after the work was done, many of the workers moved on—but not all. Some found the Grand Coulee's rugged beauty to their liking and became residents of Grant County. (Courtesy Coulee Pioneer Museum.)

Canal work would go on for many years, eventually irrigating almost 700,000 acres through 6,000 miles of canals in eastern Washington. The water came from Lake Roosevelt behind the Grand Coulee Dam on the Columbia River. (Courtesy Coulee Pioneer Museum.)

Banks Lake eventually held and distributed over 245 billion gallons of water into the vast, arid lands of the Columbia Basin, forever altering the economy and landscape. Where the waters of the prehistoric Columbia River once cascaded over the largest waterfall in history was now kept dry by the Dry Falls Dam and the Bacon Siphon. (Courtesy Grant County Historical Museum.)

Six

VIC'S FOLLY AND THE CREATION OF SUN LAKES

The late 1940s and 1950s were a golden age of recreation. The war was over, and the population once more increased as soldiers returned home from overseas. Work got started on the Bacon Siphon, and automobiles were now a way of life, as the world became more dependent on fossil fuels. Gas was cheap, and the open road called with adventure. In a time when families were more cohesive, television was rare, and the internet decades from creation, people turned to the great outdoors for entertainment. (Courtesy Grant County Historical Museum.)

Elected lieutenant governor at the same time as Franklin D. Roosevelt's landslide 1932 election, Victor Aloysius "Vic" Meyers stayed in politics and after World War II became chairman of the Washington State Parks and Recreation Commission when it switched over from being the Washington State Parks Committee in 1947. Meyers took an interest in the property below Dry Falls. Attracted to the lakes, he wanted to expand the state park to the shores of Park Lake. (Author's collection.)

Vic Meyers pushed for the name Sun Lakes because he thought it had better appeal than Dry Falls. He planned to expand Dry Falls State Park into the Lower Coulee, where the state already owned land and a few farms and private resorts were located. (Courtesy Michael Lemann.)

The land for the park was acquired through various means, with most of it having been purchased or donated to the state in the 1920s and 1930s. All of it was lumped together, giving the Sun Lakes project a starting point and room to grow. (Courtesy Coulee Pioneer Museum.)

Proposed Site of Lodge at Park Lake - July 24, '45.

The Parks and Recreation Commission also acquired Park Lake Resort, where a gas station was located. The resort sat in a cove, had an excellent sandy beach on Park Lake, and was right on the Scenic Highway. It also came with several buildings and cabins that could be repurposed. (Courtesy Dan Bolyard.)

There was a natural sandy swimming beach that had attracted people for years. The land was leveled off, and a huge parking lot was added for the new state park. The area around the beach was also cleaned up, and covered tables were added. (Courtesy Willard family.)

When it was a resort, there was one house that the resort keeper lived in across the highway from the beach and the store. The house sat on a fairly level area against the base of the coulee wall surrounded by sagebrush and nature. (Courtesy Dan Bolyard.)

The store and gas station were leased out. The gas station had all conveniences; besides being able to fuel up, customers could eat at the café and buy fishing gear or swim trunks, a soda pop, postcards, toiletries, and pretty much anything else one could think of, including motor oil and scrambled eggs. (Courtesy Willard family.)

The cabins that were moved across the highway were used for employee housing. People working in the park, as well as the people leasing the store and gas station at one time lived in the cabins and houses. There were a wide variety of people living in the park at the beginning, including official park and non-park employees. (Author's collection.)

Not everyone stayed all year; during the summer months, the people who lived in the park were busy due to the flood of tourists, but then things would slow down as soon as school started. Some of those living in the park had families; their children attended nearby Coulee City schools. (Courtesy Willard family.)

In 1947, the Parks and Recreation Commission also started work on a group of cabins across the bay from the original store. This area was set up like a resort, with a store and a laundry room. The cabins continued to grow in number as time passed. (Author's collection.)

AUTO CABINS AT PARK LAKE   SUN LAKES STATE PARK - WN   Ellis 5813

This became the Sun Lakes Park Resort. At first it was pretty basic, likely due to the short planning and construction time, with several cabins along with a laundry facility and comfort station. Eventually it grew to contain a store, café, and souvenir shop as well as a swimming pool. (Courtesy Willard family.)

Even though Vic Meyers was sometimes controversial, he was a media darling. He would hold staged events for the media and peers, trying to sell his ideas, and sometimes, it seemed to entertain the masses. The papers dubbed the whole project "Vic's Folly" and ridiculed his idea for a park in the middle of nowhere. (Author's collection.)

Regardless of the media or public opinion, the state park went on as planned. The new park would be somewhat extravagant; not only would it have campsites and lakeside activity, but also other entertainment options, like a riding stable, a golf course, multiple concessions stands, and boat rentals, as well as a new name. (Courtesy Wes and Suzy Perkinson.)

Even though the park had been called Dry Falls State Park for a couple of decades, Vic Meyers wanted to change the name to Sun Lakes State Park because he felt it reflected the new park better. This would mean changing signs, postcards, flyers, brochures, and souvenirs. (Author's collection.)

The change met with some opposition, even while the bulldozers were clearing land. Tradition is hard to break, and by this point, the name Dry Falls State Park had been around for generations and had many fans. Many people did not want to let go of the original name. (Courtesy Dry Falls Interpretive Center.)

The park officially opened in the late 1940s, drawing people from all over to swim, camp, fish, or hike in the Lower Grand Coulee. Vic Meyers's vision of a bigger state park stretched from Dry Falls down into the coulee, right up to the shore of Park Lake. (Author's collection.)

It was an immediate success, filling to capacity with visitors. The park appealed to both the summer vacationer as well as the outdoor enthusiast, with miles of lakes to fish and miles of trails to hike. (Courtesy Dry Falls Interpretive Center.)

Camping had become very popular, with people of all ages pitching tents at the newly constructed campsites. Each site had its own table and fire pit, with water and other facilities close by. Plus, once camp was set up, everything was within walking distance. (Courtesy Dry Falls Interpretive Center.)

The big attraction was the new day-use area and beach. Located right behind the cafe, the beach was a huge draw on hot summer days in the desert. It was often filled to capacity with people frolicking in Park Lake, with Umatilla watching nearby. (Courtesy Grant County Historical Museum.)

Another big attraction was fishing. On opening day, the boats on the lakes looked more like bumper cars, and the shores were lined with fishermen. There were fishing derbies put on by various organizations, and everyone wanted to get out and catch the biggest fish. There was always lots of press to cover opening day and promote the start of the season. (Courtesy Grant County PUD.)

But the beach was not the only entertainment that Sun Lakes had to offer. There was also the first golf course, Sun Lakes Golf Course, which offered vacationers and campers something to do out of the water. (Courtesy Washington State Archives.)

A new lake was created behind the campgrounds that was easy to access on foot. An earthen walkway with several offshoot paths that went nowhere were built out into the small lake; this was designed with fly fishing in mind, which was popular in the late 1940s. (Author's collection.)

The lake was then stocked with trout and named Rainbow Lake. It was well received and became a popular fishing hole for people of all ages. It was easy to access from the campground and provided a great way to start or end the day. (Courtesy Washington State Archives.)

Deep Lake also underwent a refurbishing with a new dock and parking lot. It officially became part of Sun Lakes State Park and soon was a popular place for older kids and teenagers to swim. Natural cliffs gave visitors places to dive from, and soon, Deep Lake became popular with the more adventurous. (Author's collection.)

A new restroom along with a concession stand and boat launch were added. The concession stand was seasonal and usually relied on locals for employees. Trails were developed and maintained along the side for people to fish, hike, and explore. (Courtesy Wes and Suzy Perkinson.)

Over 85 feet deep, a lot of stories rise up out of Deep Lake, like the time it boiled due to a magma event deep in the earth or that it is actually bottomless. Over the centuries, Deep Lake has been many things to many people, and one can still hear echoes of stories, legends, and rumors. (Courtesy Grant County Historical Museum.)

For most people, though, it just became a place to explore, fish, and swim. There are stories about people scuba diving the depths of Deep Lake, but the bottom mostly remains a mystery. The underwater canyon was carved out by the same water that created Dry Falls. (Courtesy Grant County Historical Museum.)

As soon as the irrigation system went in, the Sun Lakes Golf Course came to life. The course was set up above the campgrounds and looked down on Park Lake. It had a huge old clubhouse in which people could gather for a soda and get out of the heat. (Courtesy Grant County Historical Museum.)

The golf course was just one of the many grand ideas for the new park. The park Vic Meyers had in mind was more like an amusement park than what is considered a park these days. The scope of the project seemed out of place to a lot of people. (Courtesy Dry Falls Interpretive Center.)

The new Sun Lakes State Park would also have a riding stable and hired seasonal workers to take people out on horseback rides into the bottom of Dry Falls and, if they took the long ride, around Umatilla. Eventually, the riding stable moved from where it sat by the clubhouse to the entrance of Deep Lake Road. (Courtesy Wes and Suzy Perkinson.)

Sun Lakes State Park tried to keep aspects of the Wild West alive. In the 1950s, entertainers like Roy Rogers fueled everyone's imagination; this was reflected in the park, which had a natural connection with the Wild West. (Author's collection.)

The state park now hired more people than ever before and secured the whole north shore of Park Lake. People could hike, fish, boat, ski, swim, golf, camp, explore, eat a café meal, and sit around a fire. But Vic Meyers was not done and introduced white fallow deer into the environment as the final stroke of his recreation paintbrush, adding color to the hills. (Courtesy Willard family.)

The fallow deer that were introduced mostly stayed in the hills west of the park, closer to Dry Falls. Introduced as a large herd and protected from hunters, the deer population nevertheless did not fare well in its new environment, and in a few decades faded into memory. (Author's collection.)

Dry Falls was now considered part of Sun Lakes State Park and received funding for upgrades. By the 1950s, everyone had a car, and Dry Falls continued to be a popular place to stop for a quick snack, bathroom break, or leg stretch. (Author's collection.)

A concession stand was added next to the Vista House, where people could get a souvenir or drink. On hot days, the concessions stand also sold ice cream. It was leased out, and the person running it lived in the park with his wife and daughter. (Courtesy Willard family.)

By this time, cars had evolved, and the roads had to evolve to match them. One of the roads to receive a major makeover in the early 1950s was State Road 7, including the Scenic Highway portion. (Author's collection.)

The new highway was eventually named State Route 17 and ran on the west side of Park Lake instead of through the busy state park area. This was beneficial for trucks that hauled merchandise; however, it cut off Sun Lakes State Park from the highway. (Courtesy Michael Lehmann.)

The new State Route 17 continued past Dry Falls and onto Highway 2. By the late 1950s, Dry Falls had become a celebrity of sorts. Everything around it shared the name—Dry Falls Junction, Dry Falls Dam, Dry Falls Café, Dry Falls Lake, Dry Falls Cave—but even so, Dry Falls State Park itself had lost its name and was now Dry Falls in Sun Lakes State Park, with many people seeing it as its own entity. (Author's collection.)

As time went on, it became apparent that separate leases were not going to work because the people holding the lease and working or hiring could not make sufficient income, even with the busy summer tourist seasons. (Courtesy Jim and Jeanie Ping.)

During the summer, there was a flood of people, but when tourist season slowed down in the fall, so did the income. In 1958, the State Parks and Recreation Commission joined all the separate leases into a single long-term lease. (Courtesy Jim and Jeanie Ping.)

The land was still part of the state park, but after the creation of the new Sun Lakes Park Resort, the golf course, boating dock, riding stable, store, café, and cabins all came under the supervision of the leaseholder. (Author's collection.)

The lease included maintenance and some expansion of the park area but allowed freedom for Sun Lakes Park Resort to create its own events as well as modify or change existing ones, with consent and help from the leaseholder, the State Parks and Recreation Commission. (Courtesy Jim and Jeanie Ping.)

Seven

THE YEARS
THAT FOLLOWED

With funding from state- and self-generated funds, Sun Lakes State Park continued to evolve over the decades to fit the needs and desires of the people, and they kept pouring in. Dry Falls became a stop for thousands of people traveling the old Scenic Highway, now modified and renamed Highway 17. (Author's collection.)

The 1950s had been a golden era of recreation in Washington State; backed by federal money, the state park went into a land acquisition frenzy to feed the growing public demand. The number of state parks increased from 79 to around 130. The number of people visiting them jumped from 1.5 million a year to 7 million. (Author's collection.)

Backed by voter approval and federal programs, the 1960s saw Washington get a boost of financial backing and another chance to expand, develop, improve, and repair parks in the state. This statewide agenda brought repairs and improvements to Sun Lakes and Dry Falls. A new golf course clubhouse was created in 1960. (Courtesy Dry Falls Interpretive Center.)

In 1965, the National Park Service registered the entire Grand Coulee as a natural landmark. A plaque commemorating the accomplishment was placed in the heart of the Grand Coulee, in the oldest, most unmistakable part of Dry Falls: the Vista House. (Author photograph.)

The prestigious natural landmark award is presented by the secretary of the interior to outstanding sites that represent a unique quality. The whole of the Grand Coulee was recognized for its geological examples. (Author photograph.)

The year 1965 was also when Dry Falls received its first interpretive center. The square white building was designed by Spokane architect-designer Kenneth Brooks to be modernist, simple, clean, and non-intrusive. This style was popular for a very short time, and this building is one of few flawless examples left in America. (Courtesy Grant County PUD.)

The Dry Falls Interpretive Center opened to the public in 1966. The new building became a natural museum and learning center filled with displays, artifacts, and explanations. It also contained a movie room, souvenir shop, and a place for an interpretive specialist to host geological or historical events. (Courtesy Grant County PUD.)

The new interpretive center had something for everyone, including modern conveniences and air conditioning. The biggest draw for most people and probably all kids was the overlook, where visitors could gaze into Dry Falls from a new vantage point while safe behind a wall of glass. (Author's collection.)

By the 1970s, Vic's Folly had become one of the busiest parks in the state, Sun Lakes State Park, and attendance continued to soar. The park attracted people from all over the country as well as those who lived close by, offering something for everyone. (Courtesy Jim and Jeanie Ping.)

One of the big draws with Sun Lakes State Park was the social aspect. In a time before social media, people had to actually go out into the world to meet other people their age in hopes of finding common ground and socializing. (Courtesy Grant County PUD.)

Fishing had always been a big deal around the lakes in the Lower Coulee, and Sun Lakes was no different. The papers would write articles in support of opening day of the fishing season, dropping hints and clues, and when the season opened, there would be hundreds of boats out on the lakes and fisherman lining the shores. (Courtesy Willard family.)

By 1974, Sun Lakes State Park had 246 campsites that were filling to capacity every night during the summer months, causing run-offs, which, along with a few other factors, resulted in the expansion of Steamboat Rock State Park. (Courtesy Dry Falls Interpretive Center.)

In August 1977, the golf course was renamed the Vic Meyers Golf Course, and the State Parks and Recreation Commission changed the name of Rainbow Lake to Vic Meyers Lake in honor of the man whose vision made the popular vacation spot a reality. (Courtesy Wes and Suzy Perkinson.)

Vic Meyers traveled once more down into the coulee to the state park he created in the desert for the dedication ceremony. The project that had been scoffed at was now filled to capacity with people having fun and making memories. It was a complete success. A plaque was installed overlooking the swimming area in memory of Vic's Folly, and the area was dedicated to Vic Meyers. (Author photograph.)

The old store by the day-use area had become a franchise fast-food restaurant, making life easier for campers and picnickers alike. There was really no reason to leave the park anymore. One could get everything they needed to have a wonderful vacation without ever leaving the Lower Coulee. (Courtesy Jim and Jeanie Ping.)

Sun Lakes State Park became a city in the summer, with people coming from all over to work and play. The new state park has helped support the local economy with the thousands of tourists it attracts every year. (Courtesy Dry Falls Interpretive Center.)

Change is inevitable as time rolls on. The old café that had served tens of thousands of people over decades and generations eventually fell into disrepair and had to be burned. New insurance policies and regulations caused the end of the Sun Lakes Riding Stable and associated rides. (Courtesy Jim and Jeanie Ping.)

A new miniature golf course was built at Sun Lakes Park Resort. Events like the Great Canoe Race and golf and fishing tournaments were added over the years, as well as boat and paddleboat rentals, a new store, café, swimming pool, and souvenir shop. (Courtesy Jim and Jeanie Ping.)

By the 1980s, the highway had been built and rebuilt several times, leaving old, discarded bits of blacktop roadways littered around the Lower Coulee. Some of these were put to use, like the long, curvy entrance to Sun Lakes, a piece of the old Scenic Highway. (Courtesy Grant County PUD.)

The old Scenic Highway on the west side of Park Lake became gated, and its blacktop surface turned into a one-and-a-half-mile walking trail traveling almost the length of the lake. From it, one can gaze over the waters of Park Lake onto the new Highway 17, created in the 1950s. (Author photograph.)

Finally vindicated for his ideas, J Harlen Bretz was awarded the prestigious Penrose Medal at age 96 in 1979. It is the highest award one can receive as a geologist. (Courtesy Coulee Pioneer Museum.)

In 1994, the Dry Falls Interpretive Center was dedicated to J Harlen Bretz for his work in the field of geology and for helping to unlock the mysteries of the Grand Coulee and the world itself by debunking the uniformitarianism that kept scientific thought stagnant. The interpretive center was unique, created with a unique idea, much like how people saw Bretz and his ideas in the 1930s. (Author photograph.)

In 1998, the State Parks and Recreation Commission changed the name of the park from Sun Lakes State Park to Sun Lakes–Dry Falls State Park, once more returning the world's largest waterfall its own identity, even if it was now bound with the land below. (Courtesy Dennis King)

Sun Lakes–Dry Falls State Park and Sun Lakes Park Resort continue to thrive and evolve as society changes and moves forward. In 2014, Sun Lakes Park Resort started an annual classic car show that highlights some of the vehicle designs of the past, once more bringing a parade of automobiles to the coulee. It is just a small sampling of the millions of cars of all shapes, makes, and sizes that have visited Dry Falls and Sun Lakes over the decades. (Courtesy Goldey Moyer.)

Dry Falls still receives tens of thousands of visitors annually who stop to freshen up and take a look at the scenery while they stretch their legs. Dry Falls is a meeting place for many people and a getaway for others. In time, it has inspired people to great heights and sheltered people in their lows. Everyone who views it takes something with them, a memory of the brief passing moment and maybe a photograph. (Author photograph.)

Dry Falls has inspired people to take action for what they believe in, ultimately leading to the creation of Sun Lakes State Park and Vic's Folly. There are many stories that seem appropriate about Vic Meyers and a few that are probably inappropriate. One is the story of Vic Meyers and his band playing jazz on a warm, summer night in the 1950s on the shores of Park Lake. (Author's collection.)

Discover Thousands of Local History Books Featuring Millions of Vintage Images

Arcadia Publishing, the leading local history publisher in the United States, is committed to making history accessible and meaningful through publishing books that celebrate and preserve the heritage of America's people and places.

Find more books like this at
www.arcadiapublishing.com

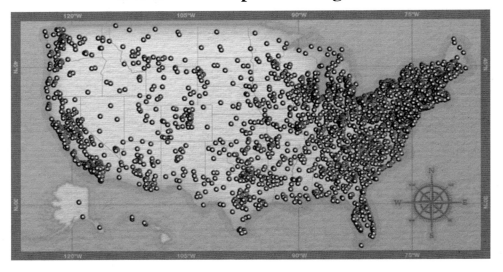

Search for your hometown history, your old stomping grounds, and even your favorite sports team.